Epics for Students, Second Edition, Volume 2

Project Editor: Sara Constantakis Rights Acquisition and Management: Margaret Chamberlain-Gaston, Savannah Gignac, Tracie Richardson, Jhanay Williams Composition: Evi Abou-El-Seoud

Manufacturing: Drew Kalasky

Imaging: John Watkins

Product Design: Pamela A. E. Galbreath, Jennifer Wahi Content Conversion: Katrina Coach Product Manager: Meggin Condino

For product information and technology assistance, contact us at **Gale Customer Support, 1-800-877-4253.**

For permission to use material from this text or product, submit all requests online at **www.cengage.com/permissions**.

Further permissions questions can be emailed to **permissionrequest@cengage.com** While every effort has been made to ensure the reliability of the information presented in this publication, Gale, a part of Cengage Learning, does not guarantee the accuracy of the data contained herein. Gale accepts no payment for listing; and inclusion in the publication of any organization, agency, institution, publication, service, or individual does not imply endorsement of the editors or publisher. Errors brought to the attention of the publisher and verified to the satisfaction of the publisher will be corrected in future editions.

Gale
27500 Drake Rd.
Farmington Hills, MI, 48331-3535

ISBN-13: 978-1-4144-7621-6 (set)
ISBN-13: 978-1-4144-7622-3 (vol. 1)
ISBN-13: 978-1-4144-7623-0 (vol. 2) ISBN-10: 1-4144-7621-3 (set)
ISBN-10: 1-4144-7622-1 (vol. 1)
ISBN-10: 1-4144-7623-X (vol. 2) This title is also available as an e-book.
ISBN-13: 978-1-4144-7624-7
ISBN-10: 1-4144-7624-8
Contact your Gale, a part of Cengage Learning sales representative for ordering information.

Printed in the United States of America
1 2 3 4 5 6 7 14 13 12 11 10

Le Morte d'Arthur

Thomas Malory 1485

Introduction

Although Thomas Malory is thought to have written *Le Morte d'Arthur* in 1469, the first known publication was in 1485 by William Caxton. In this first edition, the work was divided into twenty-one books and 506 chapters. In 1934, another manuscript version was discovered in the Fellows Library of Winchester College. This manuscript is more fully developed in sections than the earlier one and is divided into ten parts, forming five larger sections. First published in 1947, this later version is the one more commonly used. It is available in various editions, one of which is the 2010 Signet

Classic edition, titled *Le Morte D'Arthur: King Arthur and the Legends of the Round Table*.

In composing *Le Morte d'Arthur*, Malory took various legends, mostly French in origin, and adapted them to English life, with an English perspective. Malory used courtly romances about Lancelot, dating from 1225 to 1230. These stories purport to be historical accounts of King Arthur and his knights and of their quest for the Holy Grail. In addition to the French sources, Malory used material from a fourteenth-century English poem, the alliterative *Morte Arthure*. Although Arthur may have existed, little actual historical evidence survives for the stories, which are believed to derive from legend and folklore. Many scholars have attempted to prove that Malory's work is based on fact, but its attraction has tended to be the text itself with its emphasis on courtly love, honor and virtue, and, magic and miracles. *Le Morte d'Arthur* was immediately popular and has remained so over the centuries. It influenced subsequent works, including Edmund Spenser's *Faerie Queene* and Alfred Tennyson's *Idylls of the King*. *Le Morte d'Arthur: The Winchester Manuscript* was published as a paperback in 2008 by Oxford University Press; it is also available in Kindle and audio book editions and a beautifully illustrated hardback edition.

Author Biography

The authorship of *Le Morte d'Arthur* has long been disputed, although for practical purposes, the actual identity and biography of Thomas Malory has come to be less important than the literary folklore that surrounds this individual. Traditionally, *Le Morte d'Arthur* has been attributed to Thomas Malory, a knight, who was born about 1405 in Warwickshire, England. As a young man, Malory is said to have served in Calais with the forces of the Earl of Warwick, and he succeeded to his father's estate, New bold Revel in Warwickshire, in 1433 or 1434, probably when he was in his twenties. Shortly after, Malory married, although there is little reliable information about his personal life with his wife, Elizabeth. There is evidence of one child, a son, Robert, although there may have been more offspring. There are, however, accounts of Malory's imprisonment, which followed what appeared to be a fairly respectable life. After inheriting his father's estate and a second estate a few years later, Malory led a quiet and, by most accounts, affluent life, and he served as a member of Parliament. But for some reason, perhaps political ones, in about 1450, Malory was arrested. He was charged with various violent crimes but never brought to trial. When Edward IV issued a pardon for prisoners, Malory was specifically excluded.

Since it is unlikely that a knight with money and position would turn to criminal life, respected

British historian Christina Hardyment proposes in her 2007 book *Malory: The Knight Who Became King Arthur's Chronicler* that the charges against Malory were politically motivated, and his imprisonments resulted from a possible love affair gone wrong and loyalty to Henry VI. Such a view has been expressed by other critics as well. Malory died in 1471 and was buried in the cemetery at Christ Church Greyfriars, in New gate Street, in the City of London.

Malory is credited with writing *Le Morte d'Arthur* during the last years of his imprisonment. Some scholars and historians who dispute Malory's authorship, do so on the assumption that he was little more than a common thief and was, therefore, not capable of composing such an important work. There is no way to assert with complete accuracy if this Thomas Malory, or any other Thomas Malory, was actually the author of this work, but Malory's criminal record is not an indicator of his literary capabilities. *Le Morte d'Arthur* is filled with battles and details about chivalry and themes of lust and jealousy. These are all subjects that Malory, the knight turned criminal, would know about. A statement at the end of the book indicates *Le Morte d'Arthur* was completed in "the ix yere of the reygne of kyng edward the fourth." That date corresponds to the period between March 4, 1469, and March 3, 1470, near the end of Malory's imprisonment and life. *Le Morte d'Arthur* was printed in 1485 by William Caxton. There is no evidence that Malory wrote any other texts.

Plot Summary

I. The Tale of King Arthur

The birth of Arthur results from King Uther's deceptive bedding, which is really a rape, of Arthur's mother, Igrayne. Merlin, who arranges with Uther for the satisfaction of his lust, is promised the child who results. After Arthur's birth, Merlin sends the child to live with Sir Ector. Two years later, Uther dies, and Merlin secures the dying king's promise that Arthur shall be king. With Uther's death, the kingdom is in disarray with several of the barons struggling to gain control. Merlin and the archbishop arrange for a gathering of the lords. When the lords arrive, they find a sword buried in a stone. Upon the stone are the words, "whoso pulleth out this sword from this stone and anvil is duly born king of all England." None of the men present can budge the sword, but Arthur, who assumes the sword is one mislaid by Kay, easily pulls the sword free. However, the lords do not wish to be ruled by a boy and resist proclaiming Arthur king. Eventually, however, the lords agree, and as king, Arthur is successful, ruling equitably and cautiously.

When Arthur has himself crowned king of Wales, the husbands of Uther's three daughters, who are themselves kings, arrive for the coronation. However, instead of arriving to celebrate with

Arthur, kings Lot, Nantres, and Uriens arrive to make war. Although Merlin tells the three kings of Arthur's heritage and arranges a truce, Merlin returns to Arthur telling him to attack because destiny is with him. After his easy victory over his enemies, Arthur meets and falls in love with Guinevere. Arthur also creates a child, Mordred, with Lot's wife, whom Arthur does not realize is his sister. Soon, Merlin appears disguised first to tell Arthur that he is Uther's son, and later, to tell Arthur that he has lain with his sister and created a child who will destroy him. When Arthur loses his sword in battle against Sir Pellanor, Merlin leads Arthur to the Lady of the Lake, where Arthur promises a later gift in return for his sword, which will protect him as long as he wears it. In a final effort to secure his kingdom and himself, Arthur orders the deaths of all highborn children born on May Day, but the reason for this order, Mordred, survives. Instead, Arthur incurs the wrath of his lords. Merlin has had a part in every event that has shaped Arthur's life, although Arthur does not yet know it.

Media Adaptations

- The 1953 MGM film *Knights of the Round Table*, starring Robert Taylor, Ava Gardner, and Mel Ferrer and directed by Richard Thorpe, was nominated for Academy Awards in Best Art Direction/Set Directionand Best Sound.
- Originally a Broadway play, the 1967 Warner Brothers' film *Camelot*, starring Richard Harris and Vanessa Redgrave and directed by Joshua Logan, received several Academy Awards and Golden Globe Awards.
- The 2001 Turner Home Entertainment mini-series *The Mists of Avalon* was based on the book by Marion Zimmer Bradley. The story

focuses on the powerful and mystical women of the legend in the time just before Arthur be comes king.

- The 2002 video recording *Malory's "Le Morte d'Arthur": Anatomy of a Legend*, produced by Films for the Humanities and Sciences, presents three experts who analyze the epic in addition to reenactments, location footage, and related artwork.
- The 2005 Acorn Media three-part series *King Arthur's Britain* tours historical and archeological sites for clues about the state of Britain in the sixth century when Arthur was king.
- The 2006 three-part video from Kultur Video *Legend of King Arthur: Merlin, Camelot, and King Arthur* delves into history to uncover facts about Camelot and the Holy Grail and discuss the latest theories. It also reviews images in great art and other graphics that illustrate and add their own interpretations of the legend.
- The 2008 A&E Television Networks broadcast *Quest for King Arthur* explores the legend, the facts, and the state of Arthurian research.
- In the 2010 Image Entertainment

series *King Arthur & the Knights of Justice*, Merlin goes into the future to seek replacement knights from a modern football team to defend Camelot from Morgana, Lord Viper, and the Warlords after they capture Arthur and the Round Table Knights.

The story now shifts to an emphasis on revenge as a magical sword is used by a newly released prisoner, Sir Balyn, to slay the Lady of the Lake. When Sir Balyn attempts to win back Arthur's favor, he accidentally kills Launceor of Ireland, one of Arthur's men, and is responsible for the suicide of Launceor's sister. Soon another battle with King Lot ensues, Pellanor kills the king, and Arthur manages a great victory over his enemies. Merlin warns Arthur that he must guard his scabbard and that the woman to whom he gives it will steal it. Arthur gives it to Morgan le Fay, his sister, who gives the scabbard to her lover. After many battles, Balyn dies in battle with his brother, the two having killed one another by mistake. Merlin fixes Balyn's sword so that no man can use it except Lancelot or Galahad.

Against Merlin's advice, Arthur marries Guinevere. Her dowry is the Round Table, which seats 150, the seats of which Merlin fills with as many knights as he can find. One of the new knights is Lot's son, Gawain. After some minor skirmishes, Arthur establishes the new code for the Knights of the Round Table. The new code demands that the knights be merciful, righteous in their battles, and honorable toward women.

II. The Tale of Arthur and King Lucius

This book recounts the battles between Arthur and Lucius of Rome. Lucius has demanded tributes from Arthur, who refuses. Arthur promises war and is supported by his knights, who are eager for an honorable war. Although Lucius is warned of Arthur's strength, he chooses to attack anyway. Parting from his grieving Guinevere, Arthur leaves England for Normandy. The battles begin earlier than planned, after Gawain and King Bors precipitate a clash with the Romans. In spite of their lack of preparedness, Arthur's forces destroy the enemy with Gawain emerging as a heroic figure. Arthur next sends Lancelot and Cador to deliver the Roman prisoners to Paris, but Roman forces ambush them. Lancelot proves himself a hero, and the small force defeats the Romans. Lucius's men beg Lucius to end the war, but the Romans choose to attack yet again. This time, Arthur vows to take no prisoners, killing every one of his enemies in the battle. Arthur is crowned king of Rome, where he apportions the city's wealth. Soon Arthur and his men return to England and their wives.

III. The Tale of Sir Lancelot du

Lake

After his victory in Rome, Lancelot returns to England, an honored and heroic knight. This book relates Lancelot's adventures, which embody the ideal heroic knight and the code of the Round Table. In the first of the episodes related here, Lancelot is asleep under a tree when Morgan le Fay and three other ladies find him. She uses magic to return him to her castle, where the women demand that he must choose one of them or he will die. Lancelot is saved when he promises to help Sir Bagdemagus in a tournament. On his way to the tournament, Lancelot fights and wounds another knight, who had attacked him as he rested. After he wins the tournament, Lancelot is guided to Tarquin, who had earlier captured Lancelot's nephew. Lancelot kills Tarquin and has all of the prisoners released. He next kills a thief and rapist, before moving on to Tintagel Castle, where Arthur was conceived, and where Lancelot kills the giant that had been attacking women. As his adventures continue, Lancelot gives his armor to Sir Kay to protect him, and when a maiden seeks his help, Lancelot willingly risks his life to do so. He even agrees to help a lady who secretly attempts to have him killed. Soon, everyone knows of Lancelot's many heroic deeds.

IV. The Tale of Sir Gareth

Gareth is another of Lot's sons and the brother of Gawain. He is the perfect knight, more humble and pure than all the other knights. When this book begins, he is working as a kitchen boy and has adopted the name, Beaumains. Sir Kay is angered that this kitchen boy, whom he has always distrusted, is made a knight and that he is given an adventure, which is to help the maiden Lynet. However, when Sir Kay follows him, Gareth seizes Kay's spear and shield. After several adventures and the defeat of many criminal types, Gareth proves his worthiness to be a knight of the Round Table. Finally, after a tournament in which Gareth unknowingly fights his brother Gawain, Gareth is married to Lyonesse to whom he has been a devoted suitor.

V. The Book of Sir Tristram de Lyones

This book recounts the adventures of Sir Tristram,
This book recounts the adventures of Sir Tristram,
who at eighteen meets Isolde and falls in love with her. Unfortunately, he is bound to deliver Isolde to King Mark, whom Tristram serves. The love potion prepared for King Mark and Isolde is instead consumed by Tristram and Isolde, who consummate their relationship. Isolde marries King Mark, but she and Tristram remain lovers. King Mark eventually realizes what Tristram and Isolde are doing, and the two lovers flee the castle. Eventually, King Mark is able to capture Isolde, and a wounded Tristram leaves Cornwall. In Britain, Tristram meets and marries another woman, Isolde le Blaunche

Maynes, but he will not consummate the union. Tristram hears that Lancelot has condemned Tristram's betrayal of his lady.

After he again returns to Cornwall, Tristram is exiled by King Mark. Soon, Tristram encounters Arthur's knights, assists Lancelot when Morgan le Fay threatens his life, and enters a tournament. Fighting under another name, Tristram nearly wins the tournament (Lancelot wins but declares Tristram the rightful winner), but is wounded and flees to the forest. After a series of adventures, Tristram and Lancelot fight one another, although neither knows the other. Soon, the two men arrive in Camelot, where Tristram is made a knight of the Round Table. Because of Tristram's success, King Mark is more jealous than ever. He plots to have Tristram killed, but even fails at this, and when his kingdom is at risk, King Mark is forced to ask Tristram for help. Once the kingdom has been saved, King Mark writes to Arthur accusing Guinevere of faithlessness. For the remainder of this book, Tristram, Lancelot, and various other knights engage in tournaments and adventures designed to reveal their valor and strength.

VI. The Tale of the Holy Grail

Previously, Lancelot had been tricked into an affair with Elaine, the daughter of King Pelles. The child of that affair is Galahad. At the beginning of this book, there is a report that a sword has been found in a floating stone. The sword is engraved with a legend that the sword belongs to the best knight in the world, but there is also a warning that any man who tries to pull it out and fails will suffer a serious wound from it later. Gawain tries after Arthur orders him to do so, and Percival also tries to share in Gawain's curse. Galahad arrives and successfully pulls out the sword. Soon all of Arthur's knights vow to go on the Grail Quest. Galahad soon wins a white shield marked with a red cross. The story behind the shield claims that it has healing powers. Galahad undergoes many tests on his journey, and by successfully passing these tests, he proves his virtue, humility, generosity, and worthiness. Galahad is the Christ-figure, who refuses to kill his enemies but is content to drive them off. Meanwhile, Lancelot is undergoing his own tests. As a result, he learns that he has been motivated in his successes, not by love of God, but by love of Guinevere. Lancelot regrets his sins and vows to become a better man.

Percival, Lancelot, Gawain, and Bors continue their separate searches for the Grail Quest. Each man has visions while sleeping that reveal his sins. Like the other knights, these three knights are also having no luck in their search, since, as their dreams reveal, each one is too sinful to succeed. Each man understands that he is too filled with pride and lacks the humility and devotion to God that is required to succeed. Lancelot tries to enter the Grail chamber but is struck down just when he catches a glimpse of it. He lies in a coma for twenty-four days before recovering. Galahad, accompanied by Percival and Bors, finds the Grail. Galahad prays and is granted his wish of choosing his time of death. After this event, Galahad performs many miracles.

VII. The Book of Sir Lancelot and Queen Guinevere

After the Grail Quest, this book reverts to Lancelot'smore human qualities and to a life less perfect than Galahad's. Lancelot has forgotten all the promises he made during the Grail Quest and quickly turns to his love for Guinevere. Lancelot must rescue Guinevere after Meliagrance captures her. Thereafter, Lancelot is less circumspect in his loyalty and love for the queen. Lancelot has been forced to choose between King Arthur and Queen Guinevere, and he has chosen the queen.

VIII. The Death of King Arthur

It is clear to everyone that the queen and Lancelot It is clear to everyone that the queen and Lancelot are involved in an adulterous love affair. Arthur, who has ignored this betrayal for some time, can no longer ignore what has become common knowledge, and he orders Guinevere's death. As Guinevere is about to be burned, Lancelot arrives to rescue her, killing everyone who was ready to participate in her burning, including Gawain's brothers. The pope intervenes, and Lancelot returns Guinevere to the king and is banished. Gawain insists that he and Arthur attack Lancelot. This attack occurs and Lancelot wins, but refuses to kill

Gawain. While Arthur and Gawain have been pursuing Lancelot, Mordred, Arthur's incestuous son, seizes the throne and the queen. Arthur and Gawain return to fight Mordred, and Gawain dies. While discussing a truce, an error is made, and the battle resumes. Arthur kills Mordred, but in doing so, receives a fatal wound. Arthur orders Excalibur thrown into a lake, and his body is placed on a barge. Guinevere and Lancelot each turn to God in their grief, and each soon dies. Sir Constantine becomes king and the Round Table knights disperse.

Characters

Agravaine

Agravaine is a brother of Gawain and Gareth and is also a nephew of Arthur. Along with his brother, Gaheris, Agravaine participates in Mordred's plots and in the murder of his mother.

Archbishop of Canterbury

The Archbishop of Canterbury, acting in concert with Merlin, arranges for the gathering of the lords. This gathering results in Arthur's successfully pulling Excalibur from the stone and the lords' acceptance of him as their king.

Arthur

Son of Igrayne and Uther, Arthur is promised to Merlin as payment for his father's pact with the magician. After his birth, Arthur is placed in the care of Sir Ector and his son, Kay. When he is able to remove the sword from the stone, Arthur becomes king of Britain. He is wise and strong and is able to restore peace to the kingdom. However, not everyone approves of Arthur, and he must fight many battles. Finally, to secure his kingdom, Arthur orders the death of all highborn sons. This action costs Arthur much support but illustrates how far he is willing go to keep his kingdom intact. Arthur places great value on the friendship and loyalty of his men. He forms the Round Table, a forum for knightly loyalty and fealty to crown. He also establishes a code of behavior, demanding that the knights be merciful, righteous, and honorable. One of Arthur's great strengths is the loyalty he generates in his men. Even when Arthur makes a mistake in battle, his men quickly muster the strength to save both Arthur and his kingdom. He loves his knights so much that he ignores the love between Guinevere and Lancelot, until forced to act. His love for Lancelot is greater than his love for his queen. When he is forced to acknowledge his queen's love for Lancelot, he orders Guinevere burned and Lancelot banished and only undertakes to fight Lancelot because Gawain insists upon it. Arthur dies in battle with Mordred, but not until after he has killed the usurper. With Arthur's death, the Round Table dissolves, and the knights scatter.

Balyn le Sauvage

Balyn is a knight who is fated to kill his brother. In response, Merlin puts the magic sword into a stone, and it remains there until the greatest knight of the realm pulls it out.

Bors de Ganis

Bors is one of the knights who accompanies Galahad on the Grail Quest. Like Percival, Bors is one of the purest of the knights, filled with humility and valor. He is rewarded for his purity when he is permitted to join Galahad in locating the Grail. Bors witnesses Galahad's death and ascension. He returns to the Round Table and describes his visions.

Sir Ector

Sir Ector is given Arthur to raise. He is one of Arthur's brave and honorable knights who willingly goes into battle for Arthur.

Elayne

This Elayne is the daughter of King Pelles. Lancelot is tricked into an affair with this lady and they have a child, Galahad. She loves Lancelot, although he rejects her.

Elayne le Blanc

Elayne le Blanc is the maid of Astolat who loves Lancelot and who dies when he does not return her love. After her death, her body is placed on a barge with a letter telling her story placed in her hand.

Evelake

The ancient ruler, King Evelake has been promised that he will live long enough to see the virtuous knight who will complete the Grail Quest. He is four hundred years old when he dies after witnessing Galahad's successful completion of the quest.

Gaheris

Gaheris is a brother of Gawain and Gareth and is also a nephew of Arthur. Along with his brother, Agravaine, Gaheris participates in Mordred's plots and in the murder of his mother. Gaheris is ordered by Arthur to participate in the execution of Guinevere, although he is opposed and attempts to escape this duty. Gaheris is murdered by Lancelot during his rescue of Guinevere.

Galahad

The son of Lancelot, Galahad is the best of the knights, the only one capable of succeeding in the Grail Quest. He is virtuous and great enough to draw Balin's sword from the floating stone. Galahad soon wins a white shield, marked with a red cross. The shield gives him healing powers, which Galahad needs during the Grail Quest. Galahad represents a Christ-like figure. He has many adventures on his journey and encounters many enemies, but Galahad refuses to kill his enemies, content to drive them off. Galahad rejects pride and greed and refutes all seven deadly sins. Only Galahad is sinless, as is required of anyone who touches the magnificent sword and crown that he encounters on his journey. After he finds the Grail Quest, Galahad is able to perform many miracles, protected from all dangers by God and faith. Galahad is motivated only by his love of God. Eventually, Galahad sees a vision of Christ and asks to join Christ in heaven. He dies, and Percival and

Bors see Galahad ascend into heaven.

Gareth

Gareth first enters in disguise, as a humble kitchen boy, Beaumains. But he is the brother of Gawain and proves himself a brave and virtuous knight. Gareth is a gentle and virtuous knight. He is also patient and strong, the ideal of the Round Table knights. Gareth has many adventures and consistently proves himself worthy of the Round Table. Unlike many of the other knights, Gareth rejects the idea of vengeance, the spilling of blood that all the other knights appear to embrace. Gareth is ordered by Arthur to participate in the execution of Guinevere, although he is opposed and attempts to escape this duty. Lancelot, who rescues Guinevere from a sentence of death, murders Gareth. Gareth's death leads Gawain to seek revenge, which leads to his death as well.

Gawain

Gawain is Arthur's nephew, the oldest child of King Lot. He is a virtuous, just knight. Gawain emerges as a hero after he helps Arthur defeat Lucius. He errs when he beheads a lady and when he murders the unarmed Lamorak. The heroic Gawain plays the role of the loyal sidekick, for he is loyal to Lancelot. He takes the heroic central figure, though, in *Sir Gawain and the Green Knights.* Ultimately, it is Gawain's sin as murderer that prevents his complete success. When Lancelot murders Gawain's brothers,

Gawain vows revenge, and this action leads to Mordred's seizing the kingdom and the queen while Arthur and Gawain are fighting Lancelot. Gawain dies in battle, but before he dies, he admits to Arthur that his desire for revenge has led to all this calamity.

Guinevere

Guinevere is the daughter of Leodegrance and the wife of Arthur. Her dowry is the Round Table, which is filled with knights loyal to Arthur. She also represents the idea of courtly love, providing a reason for many of Lancelot's heroics. Thus, Guinevere's role is central to Arthur's success, but she is also largely responsible for his defeat. When Meliagrance kidnaps her, Lancelot appears to rescue her. Her obvious love for Lancelot leads Arthur to condemn Guinevere to death. Lancelot again rescues her as she is about to be burned. Later, with Arthur in pursuit of Lancelot, Mordred seizes Guinevere for his wife. After Arthur is killed, Guinevere enters a nunnery. After her death, she is buried next to Arthur.

Igrayne

Igrayne is the wife of the Duke of Cornwall and the mother of Arthur. She conceives Arthur after Uther comes to her bed, disguised as her husband. Igrayne has already been widowed when the disguised Uther impregnates her, and she later marries her husband's murderer.

Isolde

The daughter of Angwyssh, Isolde heals Tristram when he is wounded. Tristram loves Isolde, but King Mark claims her as his bride. When Tristram assumes the role of delivering Isolde to King Mark, the two inadvertently drink the love potion intended for King Mark and Isolde, and fall in love. They consummate their love, and Isolde continues to love Tristram even after her marriage to King Mark.

Isolde la Blaunche Maynes

This Isolde is Tristram's wife, the Princess of Brittany. Tristram refuses to consummate the marriage and makes this Isolde unhappy.

Kay

Kay is the son of Sir Ector and Arthur's foster brother. When he loses his sword, Kay sends Arthur to find it, and Arthur mistakenly pulls the magic sword from the stone. Kay is loyal to Arthur and is wounded in the battle against Lucius. Arthur is equally loyal and tolerates Sir Kay's disparaging treatment of Gareth, although Kay is clearly wrong about Gareth's abilities.

Lady of the Lake

The Lady of the Lake assists Merlin in his goals.

She demands a promise of Arthur when she

returns his sword to him. When she reappears to collect on his promise, it is to demand the head of Sir Balyn or of the maid who brought Balyn's sword. Balyn recognizes the Lady of the Lake as the woman who murdered his mother and he decapitates her.

Lamorak de Galis

Lamorak is a knight famous for his valor and his strength. Only Lancelot and Gawain are stronger. Gawain and his brother kill Lamorak because he has had an affair with their mother. Gawain cannot achieve greatness because of his role in Lamorak's death.

Lancelot du Lake

Lancelot is the greatest of Arthur's knights, except for those who succeed in the Grail Quest. He gets his first real chance to distinguish himself in the battle against Lucius, when Lancelot steals Lucius's banner. Lancelot returns to England a hero after the war in Rome. He has many adventures and proves that he is virtuous and heroic. The queen is particularly impressed with Lancelot's heroic adventures. At this point, Lancelot represents the ideal in knightly behavior, except in one area. He is clearly working to serve the queen, rather than the king. Lancelot appears to forget that he is a member of Arthur's Round Table, not Guinevere's. Lancelot joins the Grail Quest, but he has too many sins to succeed. Lancelot's knightly deeds have all been in honor of Guinevere, not God. When Lancelot finally sees the Grail, he is struck down and lies in a coma for twenty-four days and after he awakens, he returns to Camelot. Lancelot forgets that it was his love for Guinevere that prevented him from succeeding in the Grail Quest, and he quickly returns to his old ways with the queen. When Melliagaunce kidnaps Guinevere, Lancelot rescues her, and he rescues her again when she is about to be burned for adultery. His loyalty is to Guinevere and it is this misguided loyalty that helps lead Arthur to his death. After the death of Arthur, Lancelot enters the priesthood and soon dies.

Launceor of Ireland

Launceor is one of Arthur's knights. After he is humiliated by Balyn's success, he rashly attempts to defeat Balyn and is killed. Launceor's death results in severe punishment for Balyn, who dies killing his own brother.

Lynet

Lynet is a damsel who seeks Arthur's assistance. When the disguised Gareth is assigned to help her, she mocks him. However, it is this quest that proves Gareth's worthiness to join the Round Table.

Lot

Lot marries Uther's daughter. Although King Lot is the leader of Arthur's enemies, he is the most heroic of these men. He is both noble and brave and is a worthy opponent for Arthur. Two of his sons, Gareth and Gawain, become the most noble and virtuous of the Round Table knights. In order for Arthur's kingdom to be secure, Lot must finally die. He is killed in battle by Sir Pellanor, who dies himself when Gawain avenges his father's death.

Lucius

King Lucius demands tributes from Arthur, but a distracted Arthur refuses, which leads to a war. Lucius loses decisively, but he refuses to accept defeat and ignores advice to withdraw. Lucius is finally killed and the battle ends.

Mark

Mark is the king of Cornwall who, in his jealousy of Tristram, insists upon marrying Isolde, the woman Tristram loves. King Mark plots to have Tristram murdered but needs him to save his kingdom. Arthur's knights trick King Mark and generally make a fool of him, but he is really unable to do much to defend himself. An inept ruler, King Mark needs the man he hates the most—Tristram—to defend his kingdom. Mark is jealous of anyone who achieves success, even his own brother, whom he has murdered.

Melliagaunce

Melliagaunce is the traitor who kidnaps Guinevere.

When she does not yield to his demands, he accuses her of treason with Lancelot. In a fight with Lancelot, Melliagaunce is defeated and dies.

Merlin

Merlin is a master manipulator who contrives Arthur's conception and who, unseen, directs much of the action. As a great sorcerer, he is responsible for the creation of the Round Table. Both prophet and magician, Merlin is able to assume disguises and appears before Arthur disguised as both a young boy and an old man. Merlin is directly responsible for everything that happens to Arthur. Although it initially appears that Merlin represents God, it soon becomes clear that he does not, and since he does not represent God, he must, according to the medieval world, represent the devil. Merlin meets his downfall when he falls in love with Nineve, who refuses to be bedded by Merlin but is willing to study his tricks. When she has learned his magic, Nineve has Merlin sealed alive in a cave where he must remain since only she can set him free.

Mordred

Mordred is the son of Arthur's incestuous relationship with his sister. He is an evil knight, who plots to seize the crown and Arthur's queen. His actions result in a battle in which Arthur kills him. But Arthur is also killed, and the Round Table is dissolved.

Morgan le Fay

Uther's third daughter, Morgan enters school in a nunnery, becomes a necromancer, and later, marries King Uriens. Morgan le Fay attempts to steal Arthur's sword and have him murdered. She is treacherous and evil, willing to murder anyone who blocks her ambition.

Nantres

Nantres is a second king who marries one of Uther's daughters. He joins with his other brothers-in-law to fight against Arthur and is defeated.

Nineve

Nineve is the damsel of the lake and the maid Pellanor brings to court. Merlin falls in love with her and fails to see that she is using him to learn his secrets. Nineve uses magic to seal Merlin in a cave, where he must remain since no one but Nineve can free him. She uses her magic to save Arthur's life and generally uses her magic for good.

Palamides

Palamides is Tristram's enemy and Isolde's admirer. Eventually, he is forced to admit that Tristram is a worthy knight, and Palamides becomes Tristram's admirer as well.

Pellanor

Pellanor, the knight of the Questing Beast, kills Lot and is himself killed by Lot's son, Gawain. This series of murders is only one of the many that occur in an epic that focuses largely on revenge.

Pelles

King Pelles's identity is unclear, although sometimes he is the Fisher King of the Grail legends. He arranges for Galahad to be conceived and is cured when Galahad achieves the Grail Quest.

Percival le Galois

Percival is one of the more virtuous knights, who also accompanies Galahad on the Grail Quest.

Percival is raised in the woods and is lacking in everything that would be expected of a knight.

However, his desire for the Round Table is so great that he willingly sacrifices to be a knight.

Percival's desire to go on the Grail Quest means that he must repent of the pride that led him to the Round Table and of the desire to be better than Galahad. Percival has many adventures on his journey and several visions before he joins Galahad in discovering the Grail. After Galahad's death, Percival becomes a religious hermit and does not return to the Round Table.

Tristram

Tristram's experience has many parallels to that of other characters. Like Arthur, Tristram is born after his father's death and is raised by a foster parent. Like Lancelot, who loves Guinevere, Tristram loves the wife of his king. In spite of the poor treatment afforded Tristram by his king, he continues to be loyal to King Mark, returning to defend him and to save his kingdom. His love for Isolde is unabated, and even though he marries another woman of the same name, he refuses to betray the woman he loves and does not consummate the marriage. Tristram has many more adventures in which he successfully proves his strength and valor as a knight.

Uther Pendragon

Uther Pendragon is the king of primeval England. He lusts for Igrayne, who is the wife of the Duke of Cornwall. When he fails to bed Igrayne, Uther's forces attack Cornwall's, and the king then beds Igrayne while pretending to be her husband. With Igrayne's husband dead, Uther is free to marry the widow. The next two years are filled with wars and dissention for Uther, who eventually falls sick. As Uther lies dying, Merlin succeeds in convincing him to declare his child Arthur king.

Themes

Courtly Love

There are many examples of courtly love in *Le Morte d'Arthur*, including the story of Sir Gareth, his defeat of the Red Knight, and his winning of the Lady Lyonesse as his wife. Gareth represents the ideal love, one that ends in marriage and is, above all else, honorable. But the story of romantic love and chivalry that most often comes to mind is the story of Sir Lancelot and Queen Guinevere, a love that is clearly adulterous. Lancelot's heroic actions are designed to please the queen. He is clearly her favorite, and justifiably so, since in all of his adventures, Lancelot is brave, honorable, and strong. Because Lancelot fights to please and honor Guinevere, and not God, he is excluded from the quest for the Holy Grail. This depiction of courtly love changes when Lancelot is called upon to fight to save Guinevere's life. In the first instance, Guinevere is unjustly accused of murder, and a disguised Lancelot becomes her champion, overcoming Sir Mador and freeing the queen. According to romantic tradition, a knight entering a tournament might also wear a lady's token to express his love. Sir Lancelot wears the token of Elayne le Blanc, but does so only to enhance his disguise. Later, he wears the queen's token, thus making public his love for her. Another aspect of courtly love is the knight's rescue of his lady.

Lancelot has already rescued Guinevere once, but when she is kidnapped, he rescues her again from Melliagaunce, her kidnapper. Lancelot then fights and kills Guinevere's oppressor. However, because of these events, Guinevere is judged guilty of adultery and treason and is sentenced to be burned. Again, Sir Lancelot rescues his lady, but as a result, he sets into motion events that lead to the destruction of Arthur and of the Round Table. Sir Lancelot and Queen Guinevere's courtly love was far more than a harmless romantic interlude.

Honor

When Arthur establishes the code for the knights of his Round Table, one important element is honor. Arthur's knights owe him honor, but more importantly, they owe honor to God. Most of the knights waver on this last requirement. For nearly all of the knights, their adventures, battles, and tournaments are conducted in honor of their king, or more immediately, themselves. Gawain fights for personal and family honor, and Lancelot fights for the queen's honor. Because of this lack, almost all of the knights fail in their quest for the Holy Grail. Only Galahad, Bors, and Percival place honor of God ahead of personal honor, vanity, and pride. Therefore, only these three knights are permitted to complete the quest for the Grail. Malory makes individual character an important element of his story, and how each character conducts himself, in an honorable fashion, is a factor in the text.

Topics for Further Study

- Religion plays an important role in Malory's epic, often as allegory. Identify some Christian images, events, and characters in the poem and explore their influences on Arthur's court and Round Table in a class discussion. Draw illustrations that you think represent these elements or find appropriate pictures online and create a collage of Christian elements found in *Le Morte d'Arthur*.
- Contrast the images of legitimate love between Gareth and his wife and the adulterous love between Lancelot and Guinevere. Write an essay in which you describe the two and explain what you think Malory is saying about the role of legitimate

love in people's lives.

- As a classroom discussion, compile a list on the board of the elements of Arthur's Round Table code to which his knights must adhere. Then make a list separating those knights that closely follow Arthur's desires and those knights who deviate from these expectations. Defend your choices.
- Research online to find a summary of the features of the epic genre, paying special attention to the features present in Malory's poem. Create a Power Point presentation with a bullet list of standard epic features, those used by Malory and the innovative changes made by Malory.
- Explore the theme of revenge in Malory's text and how revenge ultimately leads to the destruction of Arthur's Camelot. Divide into groups, each focusing on a different incident of revenge in the story, then suggest what might have happened if the characters had not sought some other outcome.
- Using clips from various movies set in medieval times, show how jousting and sword fighting tournaments are conducted. Discuss

whether the Hollywood depiction fits your impression of these bouts from *Le Morte d'Arthur*.

Fate and Destiny

Thanks to Merlin's prophecies and his magic, many times the readers are told of a prophecy that includes death and destruction. Characters are fated to meet one another on the battlefield or in tournaments and fated to succeed or fail based on an action that occurred much earlier and for which they may have no responsibility. For example, Balyn easily draws out the sword affixed to a scabbard worn by the damsel. By doing do, he is fated to kill his dearest friend, his brother. In another example, the burial spot of Launceor is fated to be the sight of the battle between Lancelot and Tristram, two knights who love one another and who would not willingly fight one another, but who are destined to do so. This fate or destiny is not attributed to God or other spiritual forces, but instead to characters present in the text. Both Merlin and the Lady of the Lake act as representatives of fate, manipulating the characters and their actions to create a fate they predict.

Obedience

Obedience is part of the duty and responsibility that all knights owe to their king and God. Obedience to

Arthur is part of every knight's code, even when obedience results in certain death. There are several examples of obedience to Arthur's commands, even when it will bring harm to the knight. One such example occurs at the beginning of the quest for the Holy Grail, when Arthur learns of the sword in the floating stone. Arthur learns that the legend promises that only the best knight in the world can claim the sword, and if any others try to pull out the sword, they will be cursed. Lancelot refuses Arthur's order to try, but Gawain willingly obeys Arthur's order because Arthur is his king and has commanded it. In another section, Arthur orders Guinevere to be put to death. In this instance, Gawain refuses to obey his king's command, but his brothers, who also object, do obey. As a result, Gareth and Gaheris are murdered by Lancelot during his rescue of the queen.

Revenge

Much of the action in this epic is fueled by the urge for revenge. The eye-for-an-eye ethic runs through the characters' stories. For instance, Sir Pellanor kills King Lot, and Lot's son Gawain, to avenge his father's death, later kills Pellanor. In another example of revenge, Gawain and his brother Gaheris murder Lamerok, whom they accused of an adulterous relationship with their mother. This feud between Lamerok and the sons of King Lot motivates many of the sons' actions before culminating in death. Finally, it is Gawain's insistence that his brothers be avenged that leads to the destruction of the Round Table. Because Arthur and Gawain pursue Lancelot, they leave the throne and the queen unattended, and Mordred seizes both. Had Gawain been able to pass on the need for blood revenge, the battle in which he and Arthur are destroyed would not have happened. Ultimately, the theme of revenge, most particularly familial blood revenge, leads to the destruction of all that Arthur has created.

Style

Medieval Romance

Medieval romance is a type of literary work that flourished from the twelfth through the fifteenth century. The Arthurian legends, which provide much of the material for Malory's work, fall in the category of medieval romances about Britain. These romances are different from classical epics in that they focus less on heroic action and more on devotion to God and sexual love. The adventure plot concerns knights, kings, and ladies in distress, and an overriding focus is on certain courtly ideals, such as honor and valor. The medieval romance has a looser plot than the classical epic. The cycle of stories from which Malory draws in writing *Le Morte d'Arthur* consist of Old French stories. Malory took stories about Tristram and Lancelot and combined them with stories about Arthur to shape a romantic tale about a sixth-century English king.

Characters

In some ways, the characters Malory used were determined by his sources. Most of his characters are members of royalty. These characters are invested with certain traits that explain their choices and the way they resolve conflict. The framework for these characters is medieval courtly activity and the gender roles are predetermined by the historical period and the narrow upper-class rank of these individuals. Malory also included individuals with magical or fanciful powers, such as Merlin and the Lady of the Lake. Not limited by verisimilitude, Malory laced the events together using the trickery of magicians and fantasy. Nonetheless, he linked the substance of a character to the character's experience, as for example, Galahad's luck in finding the Grail being due to his saintly nature.

Foreshadowing

Foreshadowing is a literary device used to hint at the plot's eventual outcome. Foreshadowing creates expectation and tension regarding upcoming events in the story. This device is one way to build anticipation and suspense regarding the characters' future and final wellbeing. Foreshadowing in Malory's epic mostly takes the form of prophesy, which often times predicts death and destruction.

Plot

Plot refers to the sequence of events. Typically, plots have a beginning, a middle, and a conclusion, and any given action tends to affect or cause the action that follows it. Plot may also consist of a series of episodes, loosely strung together without a causal relationship between events. In *Le Morte d'Arthur*, Malory expanded on his original sources in order to create a chronologically arranged plot that covers many years. The plot depicts the birth of

Arthur, his succession to the crown, and the formation of the Round Table. The plot also depicts the many adventures of the knights, particularly the quest for the Holy Grail. The adventures may string together like unrelated episodes or digressions. Then the main plot about the Round Table resumes with the conflicts that result in the knights' dispersing.

Setting

The time, place, and culture in which the action of the story takes place is its setting. The elements of setting may include geographic location, physical or mental environments, prevailing cultural attitudes, or the historical time in which the action takes place. The location for *Le Morte d'Arthur* is mostly southwest England, and the time of the action is perhaps as early as the sixth century, during the Anglo-Saxon period.

Historical Context

A Time of War

Fifteenth-century England endured the turbulence and expense of sustained military conflict. The century began with Henry V (reigned 1413–1422) deciding to invade France. Henry found ways to justify his choice, claiming a hereditary entitlement to France and a desire to unite Europe under a Christian flag. These righteous claims allowed him to claim God endorsed this attack. As it turned out, Henry had need of God. Miserable weather and rampant dysentery hampered his invasion, but eventually Henry achieved great victories and succeeded in his quest to unite France and England.

Henry emerged from these battles as a legend, having defeated the French at the Battle of Agincourt (1415) against almost impossible odds. The heavily armored French army, which was mired in the recently plowed field, quickly fell victim to the English archers who deftly attacked from a distance. As a result, the French sustained thousands of casualties and the English relatively few. Henry gave credit to God for having been party to the English victory. More important, Henry's exploits assumed mythic proportions, perhaps reminding his people of King Arthur, whose exploits on the battlefield were legendary. To seal the comparison, Henry died soon after his victories, although not in battle as Arthur had, but of the dysentery that plagued his men during the campaign.

Compare & Contrast

- **1400s:** In 1428, the University of Florence begins offering instruction in Greek and Latin literature, in part as a way to emphasize moral values. Greek and Roman works, such as the *Odyssey* and *Aeneid*, are taught, resulting in greater interest in classical epics and promoting many new ones.

  Today: Few modern authors aspire to writing epics. However, the epics of Malory and others continue to be studied. Malory's epic provides source material for film dramatizations and for archeological research.

- **1400s:** The Hundred Years War between England and France begins in the late 1330s and continues until England is defeated in the late 1450s. After the glorious victories of Henry V, there is little for the English to cheer about. In bringing the heroic Arthur to life, Malory offers the English a reason to remember their heroic past.

Today: Great Britain is a leader in world affairs. The Allied victory in World War II affirms its important global role. It participates in NATO and is a member in the European Common Market and the United Nations (with a permanent seat on the Security Council).

- **1400s:** The castle ruins at Tintagel on the north shore of Cornwall mark the site of a medieval stronghold, traditionally associated with the Arthurian legend, but now suffering from surf and weather erosion and general neglect.

  Today: Tintagel Castle, near the village of Tintagel, Cornwall, is a protected archeological site and tourist destination operated by the English Heritage.

During Malory's lifetime, English life was marked by political dissension and war. The monarchy squandered the country's wealth by waging wars when what England needed was economic recovery and stability. Except for the brief period of glory that the English enjoyed with Henry V, there had been little to cheer the people for a hundred years or more. The Peasants' Revolt of 1381, which had been caused by the imposition of a poll tax, had offered no lasting lessons for the monarchy. The revolt was squashed in less than a month, a failed revolution, so the problems that had led to the revolt were ignored. The Peasants' Revolt was about much more than the poll tax. There was a shortage of laborers and thus a shortage of food since the last serious outbreak of plague in the middle of the fourteenth century, which killed one-third of England's population. Many people were starving, and the aristocracy's solution was to raise taxes and fight among themselves for the Crown. In short, the medieval period was a time of social unrest and disorder. In spite of severe economic conditions, the Hundred Years War raged on, until finally the English were ousted from French territories. Back in England, the aristocracy was more involved with the getting and keeping of land and wealth than with responding to the needs that prompted social unrest.

Late Medieval Life

Henry VI (reigned 1422–1461) established Eton College (1440) and King's College, Cambridge (1441). These actions demonstrated the king's interest in education. But education served the aristocracy and not the needs of ordinary people. Then, too, the king's relatives had been engaged in almost constant feuds since the date of his birth, finally erupting into civil war in 1453 with the birth of Henry's heir, an event that ignited the Thirty Years War. During this period, the Crown shifted several times between the House of York and the House of Lancaster. Each side had its dissenters and its supporters, but both of these groups were quick to shift allegiance with changing military tides. While the fighting persisted, the condition of English peasants remained unchanged. The feudal system offered little benefit to those below the rank of the aristocracy. Peasants owned neither themselves nor their property. Absolute control resided with the landowner, who simply increased demand of his workers when he needed additional capital. As the poor suffered, the wealthy became even richer. This condition culminated in another peasants' revolt in 1450 and a peasants' march on London. Although some small blood shed occurred, there was little practical change.

The influence of the Hundred Years War and the English civil wars led to increased lawlessness. Stealing increased. Merchants were dishonest, selling shoddy goods and cheating their customers. The law was corrupt, with bribery the rule more than the exception. The seas were filled with pirates and the highways with robbers. Greed motivated much of what passed for English social activity. There was little to stop the common criminal.

In the late medieval period, the Catholic Church was the center of community life. Its precepts guided many people's actions, and its rules worked to curb antisocial behavior, despite the fact that Church services were conducted in Latin. An unchallenged authority, the Catholic Church maintained a strong hold on English life until the beginning of the sixteenth century. Then the first stirrings of the Reformation began in Europe, and the preeminence of the Catholic Church in England ended during the reign of Henry VIII (1509–1547).

The end of the fifteenth century marked the end of the medieval period in England. The sixteenth century brought with it the first of the Tudor kings and a period of relative peace and reduced threat from the bubonic plague. In short, England at the beginning of a new century had become a more stable place. The first of the Tudor kings, Henry VII (reigned 1485–1509), formed alliances with neighboring countries and trade flourished in London. The cloth for which English sheep were so famous became an important trade commodity in Europe.

However, the coming of trade changed the face of England. Instead of a largely agrarian society, England shifted toward trade and urban development. Land for agricultural use was enclosed, and displaced rural families fled to the larger cities where crowding, unemployment, and communicable disease were problems. Literacy gradually increased, too, as moveable type made books and other printed material more affordable and as more people learned to read.

Critical Overview

Malory's epic *Le Morte d'Arthur* deviates from traditional epics in that it is written in prose instead of poetry. This choice may reflect Malory's own talents and preference. It may also suggest his limited knowledge of classical epics. Indeed, there is little reason to think that Malory had any access to the epics such as the *Odyssey* and the *Aeneid.* The Greek and Roman epics were rare until they were *rediscovered* during the Renaissance, when they were translated and more widely distributed.

There is no evidence that Malory wrote any other works, but that does not diminish his accomplishment in producing *Le Morte d'Arthur.* With this work, Malory functioned as a compiler of the stories drawn from Arthurian legends. He assembled them in one book and imposed upon them a chronological arrangement. As Thomas Leitch noted in a comparison of the King Arthur and Robin Hood stories, Malory translated, combined, and reorganized several English and French romances. Leitch added that Malory cut long passages of theological rumination from the Vulgate cycle of Arthurian tales and disentangled the Arthur's knights in order to spotlight each one's exploits as a separate adventure. Thus Malory changed the form and effect of the stories to make them more appealing to a secular audience.

Initially, many of Malory's readers focused on

proving or disproving the historical veracity of his work. After all, in the first printing, William Caxton devoted a considerable portion of his preface to arguing that Malory's work proved that King Arthur had existed and that his exploits were historical events. However, scholarship soon showed the dearth of evidence supporting an historical Arthur; perhaps Caxton was serving more as salesman than historian. It made little difference anyway since the book helped to establish a national heritage, which had its own value.

With its emphasis on values, Malory's text implies that the English needed to read about the virtuous path emphasized by *Le Morte d'Arthur*. Arthur's establishment of the Round Table suggests perhaps a current longing for equality in civic representation and government. While many modern readers would recognize that Malory is suggesting a moral code, not all of Malory's early readers must have embraced this view. In *The Scholemaster*, for example, Roger Ascham condemns the morality of Arthur's knights, saying that books of chivalry were written by Catholic monks who enjoyed violence and lewdness.

In addition to the obvious attacks on the Catholic Church, which were common in many English texts printed after the Reformation, Ascham criticized the knights' behavior. Interestingly, this is the same criticism Malory implies. Only the purest of the knights—Galahad, Bors, and Percival—succeed in the Grail Quest. The implication is clear: Those knights who engage in adulterous behavior or who use their strength or talent with a sword in an unjust manner, cannot receive God's blessing.

Although Malory's epic was popular as entertainment, quasi-history, or even a model of morality, it was not regarded as serious literature for some time. Eventually, however, *Le Morte d'Arthur* took its place in the literary canon and was recognized as a major influence on many of the poets who followed Malory such as Spenser and Tennyson. According to Catherine Phillips in an article for *Victorian Poetry*, Tennyson knew all three of the English editions of Malory's epic that had been published in the romantic period. Additional editions appeared as Tennyson worked on his own version of the Arthurian legends: Thomas Wright's of 1858 and James Knowles' in 1862, which because of its popular modern translation was reprinted seven times by 1892, the year of Tennyson's death. *Le Morte d'Arthur* created a Victorian interest in the world of knights, jousts, and courtly love. In the twentieth century the Knights of the Round Table inspired several films and even a musical. In addition, comparisons during the presidency of John F. Kennedy to Arthur's Camelot, recalled the vitality and ideals of Arthur's rule, and after Kennedy's presidency had ended so abruptly, the brevity of such a world.

Sources

Ascham, Roger, *The Scholemaster*, Bibliolife, 2008.

Caxton, William, "Caxton's Preface," in *The Works of Thomas Malory*, Vol. 1, edited by Eugene Vinaver, Clarendon Press, 1947.

Hardyment, Christina, *Malory: The Knight Who Became King Arthur's Chronicler*, HarperCollins, 2005.

Kennedy, Edward Donald, "Malory's Guinevere: 'A Woman Who Had Grown a Soul,'" in *Arthuriana*, Vol. 9, No. 2, Spring 1999, pp. 37–45.

Leitch, Thomas, "Adaptations without Sources: *The Adventures of Robin Hood*," in *Literature Film Quarterly*, Vol. 36, No. 1, 2008, p. 27.

Lewis, C. S., "The English Prose 'Morte,'" in *Essays on Malory*, edited by Walter Oakeshott et al., Clarendon Press, 1963, pp. 7–28.

Malory, Thomas, *Morte d'Arthur: King Arthur and the Legends of the Round Table*, Signet Classic, 2010.

Phillips, Catherine, "Charades from the Middle Ages: Tennyson's *Idylls of the King* and the Chivalric Code," in *Victorian Poetry*, Vol. 40, No. 3, 2002, p. 241.

Saul, Mary Lynn, "Courtly Love and the Patriarchal Marriage Practice in Malory's *Le Morte d'Arthur*," in *Fifteenth Century Studies*, Vol. 24, September

1998, pp. 50–62.

Further Reading

Fenster, Thelma S., ed., *Arthurian Women: A Casebook*, Garland, 1996.

> This book presents essays that focuses on the women in Malory's text.

Field, P. J. C., *The Life and Times of Sir Thomas Malory*, D. S. Brewer, 1999.

> Field's book explores the evidence about Malory and attempts to establish the real identity of the author of this epic.

Hodges, Kenneth, *Forging Chivalric Communities in Malory's "Le Morte D'Arthur,"* Palgrave Macmillan, 2005.

> This book examines how Malory presents chivalry as a form of English nationalism, as a code created by large and small communities for their own purposes, and as a dynamic, continually developing ideal that, in turn, shaped the people who followed the code. Hodges includes a discussion of women's role in chivalry.

Shepherd, Stephen H. A., ed., *Le Morte d'Arthur*, Norton Critical Edition, Norton, 2003.

The Norton Critical Edition is a handy all-inone edition, with introduction, annotations to the text, and criticism designed to facilitate comprehension and appreciation of the epic.

Suggested Search Terms

Le Morte d'Arthur

King Arthur

Thomas Malory

Lancelot

Queen Guinevere

Knights of the Round Table

medieval romance

Lightning Source UK Ltd.
Milton Keynes UK
UKHW020637230222
399120UK00009B/515

9 781375 399500